SCHIRMER'S LIBRARY
OF MUSICAL CLASSICS

Vol. 1977

LUDWIG VAN BEETHOVEN

Sonatina Album

For Piano

ISBN 978-0-7935-2023-7

G. SCHIRMER, Inc.

DISTRIBUTED BY

HAL•LEONARD®
CORPORATION

7777 W. BLUEMOUND RD. P.O. BOX 13819 MILWAUKEE, WI 53213

Table Of Contents

Page

1   Sonatina in E♭ Major

9   Sonatina in F Minor

17   Sonatina in D Major

29   Sonatina in C Major

35   Sonatina in G Major

37   Sonatina in F Major

41   Sonatina in G Minor
     (Sonata op. 49, No. 1)

49   Sonatina in G Major
     (Sonata op. 49, No. 2)

Dedicated to the Princely Archbishop of Cologne, Maximilian Friedrich

SONATINA IN E♭ MAJOR

Ludwig van Beethoven
Composed in 1781

Allegro cantabile

Andante

Rondo vivace

Dedicated to the Princely Archbishop of Cologne, Maximilian Friedrich

SONATINA IN F MINOR

Ludwig van Beethoven
Composed in 1781

Larghetto maestoso

Andante maestoso

Allegro assai

12

Andante

SONATINA IN D MAJOR

Ludwig van Beethoven
Composed in 1781

Allegro

MENUETTO
Sostenuto

VAR. I

22

VAR. IV.

VAR.V.

VAR. VI

SCHERZANDO
Allegro, ma non troppo

Dedicated to Eleonore von Breuing

SONATINA IN C MAJOR

Ludwig van Beethoven

Adagio

*Completed from this point on by F. Ries.

SONATINA IN G MAJOR

Ludwig van Beethoven

Moderato

36

ROMANZE

SONATINA IN F MAJOR

Ludwig van Beethoven

Allegro assai

RONDO
Allegro

SONATINA IN G MINOR

(Sonata op. 49, No.1)

Ludwig van Beethoven

Rondo
Allegro

SONATINA IN G MAJOR
(Sonata op. 49, No. 2)

Ludwig van Beethoven

Allegro ma non troppo

Tempo di Menuetto